LIVING IN
EUROPE

Living in
France

Annabelle Lynch

W

FRANKLIN WATTS

LONDON•SYDNEY

Franklin Watts
First published in Great Britain in 2016 by The Watts Publishing Group

Credits
Series Editor: Julia Bird
Series Designer: D.R. ink

ISBN 978 1 4451 4838 0

Printed in China

Franklin Watts
An imprint of
Hachette Children's Group
Part of The Watts Publishing Group
Carmelite House
50 Victoria Embankment
London EC4Y 0DZ

An Hachette UK Company
www.hachette.co.uk

www.franklinwatts.co.uk

Contents

Words in bold are
in the glossary on
page 23.

Welcome to France!

Bonjour! I live in France.

Where is France?

France is the second biggest country in Europe. It shares **borders** with eight different countries, including Belgium, Germany, Italy and Spain. It has long **coasts** along the Atlantic and the Mediterranean.

What does France look like?

In the north and west, France is mostly flat, with some rolling hills. In the south and east are snowy, rugged mountains. Long rivers criss-cross all of France.

Belgium
Germany
Luxembourg
Seine
PARIS
Atlantic Ocean
Loire
FRANCE
Switzerland
LYON
Alps
Italy
TOULOUSE
Massif Central
Rhône
Pyrenees
MARSEILLE
Monaco
Andorra
Mediterranean Sea
Corsica
Spain

Mont Blanc is the highest mountain in France.

Snow in Paris

What's the weather?

France is so big that the weather can be quite different in the north and the south! The north has cool winters and warm summers. The south is warmer all year round, but can be wet in winter.

People in France

I come from France. People who come from France are called French.

A home in France

Around 64.5 million people live in **mainland** France. Two or three million more French people live in France's overseas territories (see pages 10–11). Over the years, many people have come to live in France from countries all over the world, including Vietnam and Algeria.

Religion

Many people in France follow the **Roman Catholic** religion. A smaller group of people are **Muslims**, many of whom brought their religion with them when they came to live in France. Around a quarter of people living in France don't follow any religion.

Where people live

Most people in France live close to a city, such as the **capital** city, Paris. Cities offer them more jobs and places to live. Fewer people live in the countryside and in the mountains.

Religion in France

Christian (Roman Catholic): 43 million

Muslim: 5 million

Other religions: 1 million

No religion: 16 million

(approximate figures)

Cities

There are lots of cities in France, but Paris, where I live, is the biggest city by far.

Belle Paris

Paris is found in the north of France. It is named after a group of people, the Parisii, who settled there over 1,700 years ago. Today, over twelve million people live in and around Paris. Millions of **tourists** also visit France's capital city every year to go to its world-famous **museums**, restaurants and shops.

The River Seine flows through Paris.

Marseille Old Port

Marseille

Marseille is the second biggest city in France. It lies in the south, on the Mediterranean Sea, and is an important **port**. Ships set sail from Marseille to travel all over the world, carrying **goods** such as oil, glass and plastics.

Toulouse

Toulouse is found in the south-west of France. It is known as the 'pink city' because many of its old buildings were built with **terracotta** bricks. Today, Toulouse is the headquarters of Airbus, the French aircraft company. The biggest space centre in Europe is also found there.

Toulouse

Islands and overseas territories

I live on the island of Corsica. Although it lies off the coast of France in the Mediterranean Sea, it is seen as part of France.

Corsica

Around 320,000 people live in Corsica all year round, but it is very popular with tourists in the sunny spring and summer. They visit Corsica to enjoy its beautiful beaches or to hike in its rocky mountains.

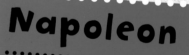

Napoleon

The famous French emperor Napoleon Bonaparte (1769—1821) was born in Ajaccio, Corsica's biggest city.

Overseas territories

Much further away from France lie France's overseas territories. These date back to a time when France had many **colonies** around the world. These overseas territories are mostly islands, apart from French Guiana, and are dotted around the Atlantic, Pacific and Indian Oceans.

French Guiana

French Guiana is found on the north Atlantic coast of South America. The land is low-lying and mostly covered in thick tropical **rainforest**.

Carnival dancers in French Guiana

volcano

Réunion

The island of Réunion lies in the Indian Ocean. It is surrounded by clear seas, and covered in thick forest. In the middle of the island is the Piton de la Fournaise volcano, one of the most active volcanoes in the world.

Mountains

France has an amazing seven mountain ranges. The most famous of these are the Alps and the Pyrenees.

The Alps

The Alps are the longest and highest mountains in Europe, stretching for over 1,000 kilometres from the Mediterranean Sea in the west to Slovenia in the east. They were formed over 300 million years ago. In France, the Alps lie close to the borders with Switzerland and Italy.

Mountain weather

The mountains are usually colder and wetter than other places in France, although they often have fine summer days. In winter it often snows. People come from all over the world to ski and snowboard in France's mountains.

The Pyrenees

The Pyrenees spread over about 500 kilometres across the south-west of France, dividing France from Spain. The tiny country of Andorra is found in between the two in the eastern Pyrenees. Though not as high as the Alps, the Pyrenees are rich in waterfalls and rare wildlife, such as the Pyrenean desman.

Pyrenean desman

What we eat

French food is the best in the world! Well, we think so anyway.

Crazy about cheese

Over 500 different types of cheese are made in France.

Eat fresh

French people love to eat fresh food and their meals often depend on which meat, vegetables and fruit are fresh and available.

Breakfast

French people often start the day with some crusty *baguette* or a pastry, such as a *croissant* or a *pain-au-chocolat*.

croissant

Lunch

Lunch is **traditionally** the main meal of the day. At school, children have a long lunch break and often go home to eat with their family. Lunch can be four courses long – soup or salad, a hot dish of fish or meat, cheese and maybe even a dessert. No wonder it takes a while to eat!

Coq au vin

Special foods

Some foods and meals are special to France. Try *bouillabaisse* – a tasty fish soup from the south of France. *Coq au vin* is a popular dish of chicken cooked with wine, garlic and bacon. Finish with an apple tart, cooked upside down, called *tarte tartin*.

A family sits down for dinner in the French Alps.

Surfing at Biarritz

Having fun

We love having fun in France! We spend lots of time outside, both in summer and in winter. We also love watching and playing sport.

Pétanque
....

Lots of people enjoy the traditional French game of pétanque. The aim of the game is to throw or roll your ball as close as you can to a smaller wooden ball.

Sunny days

In summer, French people like to visit the seaside. In the north, the beaches are wide and flat with high **cliffs** – perfect for exploring and building sandcastles. But watch out, the sea can be cold! In the south, the Mediterranean coast has lots of lovely beaches and warmer water. Along the west coast, there are big waves – great for surfing.

ski lessons

Snowy days

In winter, we head to the mountains to have fun in the snow. Skiing and snowboarding are really popular and lots of children have lessons.

Sport

Football is the most popular sport in France and thousands of fans follow the teams in League One, such as Paris Saint-Germain (PSG) and Olympique Marseille. Tennis, rugby and cycling are also very popular, both to watch and as a hobby. Every summer, we gather to watch the famous Tour de France cycling race across France.

The Tour de France

Famous places

France has lots of wonderful places to visit, both old and new.

Tall tower

The 324-metre-tall Eiffel Tower is found in the heart of Paris. It was built in 1889 and is made of strong iron. Today, you can climb right to the top of the 1,665 stairs to enjoy amazing views of Paris. Or you can take the lift!

Money maker

The Eiffel Tower is the most visited paid-for attraction in the world. Almost seven million people visit it every year.

← Versailles

The magnificent palace of Versailles, once home of the kings and queens of France, is around twenty kilometres south of Paris. It has over 700 rooms, 67 staircases and more than 2,000 windows!

Disney magic →

Disneyland Paris opened in 1992 and is now the most visited **theme park** in Europe. Try the thrilling rollercoaster ride Space Mountain or relax on a boat ride around 'It's a Small World'.

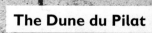

Sleeping Beauty Castle, Disneyland Paris

Sandy mountain

On the Atlantic coast, you can visit the biggest sand **dune** in the world – the Dune du Pilat. If you can climb the 107 metres to the top, you may even be lucky enough to see dolphins play in the nearby Bay of Arcachon.

The Dune du Pilat

Festivals and special days

We celebrate many of the same festivals in France as in the rest of the world, such as Christmas. Some festivals are special to France, though.

Bastille Day

Every year on 14 July, French people celebrate Bastille Day. This is a day on which they remember the events of the **French Revolution**, and celebrate the French people. Everybody has the day off. There are parades, concerts and firework displays. It is great fun!

Light show →

The beautiful Festival of Lights in held over four days every December in the city of Lyon. People light candles and lamps and place them in their windows. There are also spectacular light shows and many buildings are lit up.

Food fun

French people love celebrating food! Some more famous festivals include the Citrus Festival, held every February in the town of ← Menton. In October, Honfleur's Shrimp Festival attracts thousands of people to watch or take part in the great shrimp-peeling competition!

France: Fast facts

Capital: Paris

Population: 64.5 million

Area: 643,801 square km

Official language: French

Currency: Euro

Main religions: Christianity (Roman Catholic), Islam, Judaism

Longest river: The Loire

Highest mountain: Mont Blanc

National holidays: New Year's Day (1 January), Easter Monday, Labour Day (1 May), Ascension Day, Victory in Europe Day (8 May), Pentecost Monday, Bastille Day (14 July), Assumption Day (15 August), All Saints' Day (1 November), Armistice Day (11 November), Christmas Day (25 December)

Glossary

border a line that divides two countries

capital the city in which the government of a country meets

cliff a rocky hill near the sea

coast where the land meets the sea

colony a country that is controlled by another country

dune a hill made of sand

emperor a man who rules over a group of countries that make up an empire

French Revolution a time when the people of France rose up to overthrow their king

goods things that people can buy or sell

mainland the main part of a country, rather than the islands around it

museum a place where you can look at old and interesting things

Muslim describes someone who follows the religion of Islam

port a place by the sea from where boats and ships arrive and depart

rainforest thick forest found in places where it rains a lot

Roman Catholic a branch of Christianity that has the Pope as its head

terracotta a pink-brown clay

theme park a big, outdoor amusement park, with rides and other attractions

tourist someone who visits a place on holiday

traditional describes things that have been done in the same way for a long time

Index